WHAT I FEEL

I AM SAD

Beth Gottlieb

I0893810

first concepts

Gareth Stevens PUBLISHING

I am sad.

I want to go to the park.
It is raining.
I am sad.

I tell Mom.
We make a tent.
I feel better.

I lost my bear.

I am sad.

I cry.

Nana hugs me.
We look for my bear.

Jen moves away.
I miss her.
I am sad.

I call Jen.
We are still friends.
I feel better.

My toy breaks.
I am sad.

Dad can fix it!

I am not sad.

It is OK to feel sad.
It is OK to cry.
Everyone does
sometimes!

What makes
you feel sad?

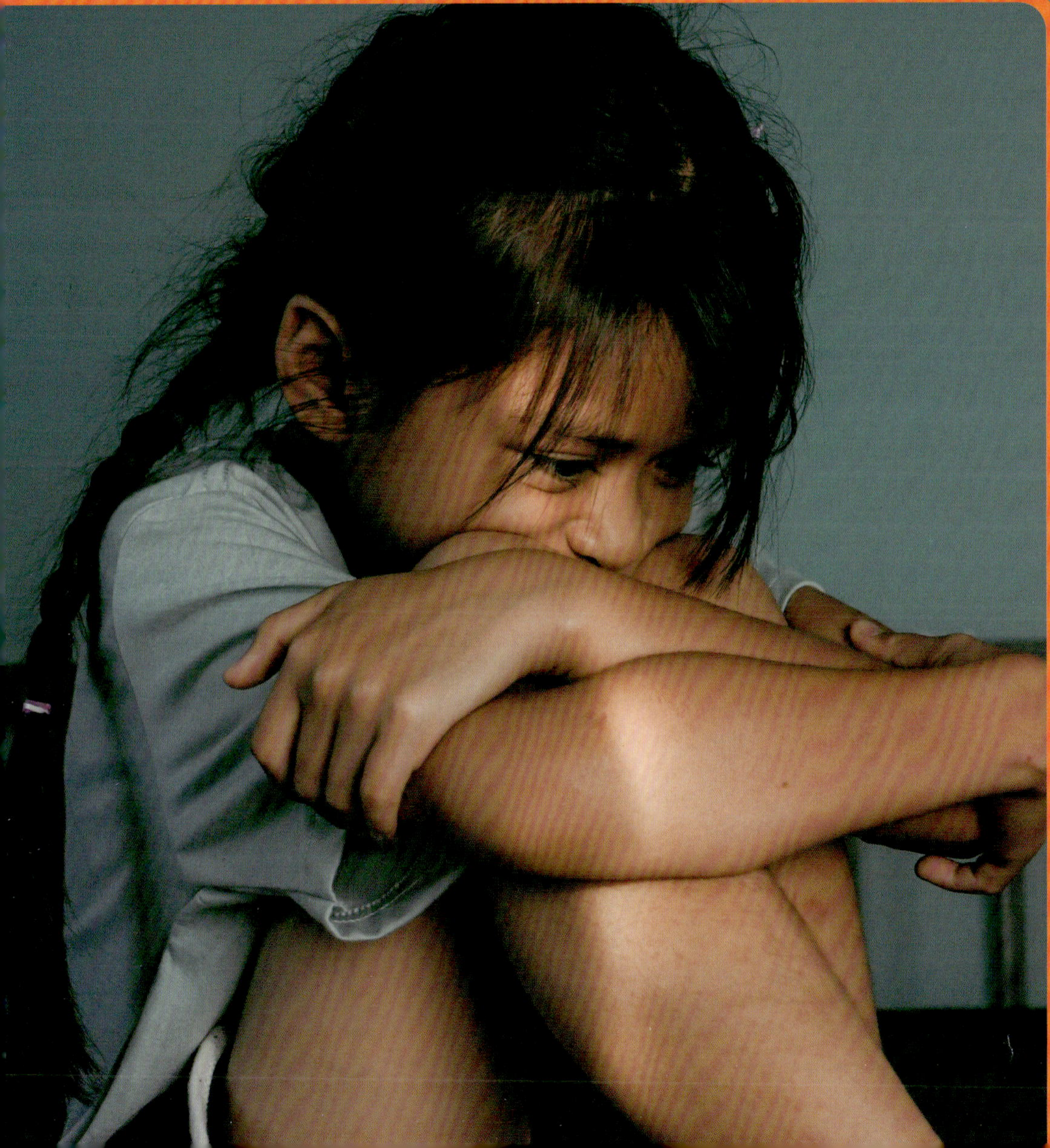

Please visit our website, www.garethstevens.com. For a free color catalog of all our high-quality books, call toll free 1-800-542-2595 or fax 1-877-542-2596.

Library of Congress Cataloging-in-Publication Data

Names: Gottlieb, Beth author
Title: I am sad / Beth Gottlieb.
Description: Buffalo, New York : Gareth Stevens Publishing, [2027] | Series: What I feel
Identifiers: LCCN 2025027215 (print) | LCCN 2025027216 (ebook) | ISBN 9781482476125 (library binding) | ISBN 9781482476118 (paperback) | ISBN 9781482476132 (ebook)
Subjects: LCSH: Sadness in children–Juvenile literature | Sadness–Juvenile literature | Emotions in children–Juvenile literature | LCGFT: Literature
Classification: LCC BF723.S15 G68 2027 (print) | LCC BF723.S15 (ebook) | DDC 155.4/124–dc23/eng/20250808
LC record available at https://lccn.loc.gov/2025027215
LC ebook record available at https://lccn.loc.gov/2025027216

Published in 2027 by
Gareth Stevens Publishing
2544 Clinton Street
Buffalo, NY 14224

Copyright © 2027 Gareth Stevens Publishing

Designer: Deanna Lepovich
Editor: Therese Shea

Photo credits: Cover Tartila/Shutterstock.com; cover, pp. 3, 5, 7, 9, 11, 13, 15, 17, 19, 21, 23 (texture) v_kulieva/Shutterstock.com; p. 3 fizkes/Shutterstock.com; p. 5 Irina WS/Shutterstock.com; p. 7 New Africa/Shutterstock.com; p. 9 Simplylove/Shuttertstock.com; p. 11 Evgenia V/Shutterstock.com; p. 13 Penyushkina/Shutterstock.com; pp. 15, 21 Prostock-studio/Shutterstock.com; p. 17 Standret/Shutterstock.com; p. 19 Yakimova Elena/Shutterstock.com; p. 23 AnnGaysorn/Shutterstock.com.

All rights reserved. No part of this book may be reproduced in any form without permission in writing from the publisher, except by a reviewer.

Printed in China

CPSIA compliance information: Batch #QSGS27: For further information contact Gareth Stevens at 1-800-542-2595.

Find us on